HAiKUS
FOR
SLEEPY
BiRDS

SUE WHITMER

HAIKUS FOR SLEEPY BIRDS

For sleepy birds everywhere

Sleepy Hummingbirds

Tired from their journeys

Hummingbirds settle down now

So sleepy tonight.

Sleepy Swans

Sleeping on water

Pond-floating sleepy white swans

Tuck beaks between wings.

Sleepy Perchers

Sleepy perching birds
Leg tendons firmly clasping
Birds can stay asleep.

Sleepy Songbirds

Hiding in the brush

Sleepy songbirds cover up

Safely for the night.

Amazing Brain Birds

Half-asleep birds with

Special brains keep well alert

Even though resting.

Upside-down Birds

Sleeping upside down
Is a quite amazing feat!
Good-night, sleepy birds.

Special thanks to
Kathryn Gile and Kathleen Whitmer.

Since she was a child, Sue Whitmer has always loved birds and poetry. She combines these passions in *Haikus for Sleepy Birds*, her first children's poetry book.

Her debut title, *Collecting Dreams*, was the #1 Hot New Release in Amazon's OCD category. The book provides personal perspective on life with a hoarder and has been used for classroom instruction at two Midwestern universities.

Sue Whitmer lives in New Jersey with her husband, Scott. The couple have two grown, married sons and two grandchilren.

The End

Made in the USA
Columbia, SC
25 June 2023

19238376R00015